Meliorism

MIMI

STARDOM BOOKS

www.StardomBooks.com

STARDOM BOOKS, LLC
112, Bordeaux Ct,
Coppell, TX 75019

Copyright © 2023 by Mimi

This book is copyright under the Berne Convention.
No reproduction without permission.
All rights reserved.

The right of Mimi to be identified as the author of this work has been asserted by her in accordance with sections 77 and 78 of the Copyright, Designs and Patents Act, 1988.

FIRST EDITION MARCH 2023

STARDOM BOOKS

A Division of Stardom Alliance
112, Bordeaux Ct,
Coppell, TX 75019

www.stardombooks.com

Stardom Books, United States
Stardom Books, India

The author and publishers have made all reasonable efforts to contact copyright-holders for permission, and apologize for any omissions or errors in the form of credits given. Corrections may be made to future editions.

Meliorism

Mimi

p. 115
cm. 13.5 X 21.5

Category:
POE023010: POETRY / Subjects & Themes / Death, Grief, Loss
POE023060: POETRY / Subjects & Themes / Political & Protest

ISBN: 978-1-957456-19-5

DEDICATION

Mom, Dad & Sam, thank you for believing in me. My beloved grandparents and family for the never-ending support. To my mentor, Ms. Yuvika, for showing me the greater and hidden side of things. Mina and Ranavir, love from the bottom of my heart (You both owe me a long hug after this).
I would sincerely like to thank my illustrator, Mithila for bringing my thoughts to life alongside my perspective of the words I write in a more imaginative way.
To those who choose to read, to change, and to have faith in the better things to come after the realisation.

CONTENTS

	Acknowledgments	i
1	Mere Idiots	3
2	Bloom Rise	5
3	The Vast Void	7
4	Froid Friend Puzzle	9
5	The Sorrows of Humanity	11
6	Neutral Times	13
7	Deceptions Misheard	15
8	The One-Way Sail	17
9	Righted Wrongs	19
10	Elevator	21
11	Thee Blossomed, I Wilted	23
12	Rusted Coins	25
13	Reflection	27
14	Magnum Opus	29
15	Sight Sighing	31
16	End Cycle	33
17	Era's Finest Knave	35
18	Man Made Malice	37
19	Yin and Yang	39

20	Burdened Baggage	41
21	The Path In-between	43
22	~~Hero~~ Villain's Arc	45
23	Woesome Witch	47
24	After Death No Life Ahead	49
25	Haunted House	51
26	Endless Infinity	53
27	Lacuna	55
28	W Women, L1964	57
29	Time Turns to Trees	59
30	The Tree, The Witness	61
31	Obscure for Sight	63
32	The Solitary Man	65
33	Pawn	67
34	Far Fetched Forest	69
35	Mundane	71
36	Quest of Time	73
37	People Pleaser	75
38	I Like Being Young	77
39	Poetry Explication	79

ACKNOWLEDGMENTS

To the people around me, I will forever be grateful to have my eyes opened to all the truths you've unveiled to me. Bitter and sour, I have nothing but gratitude.

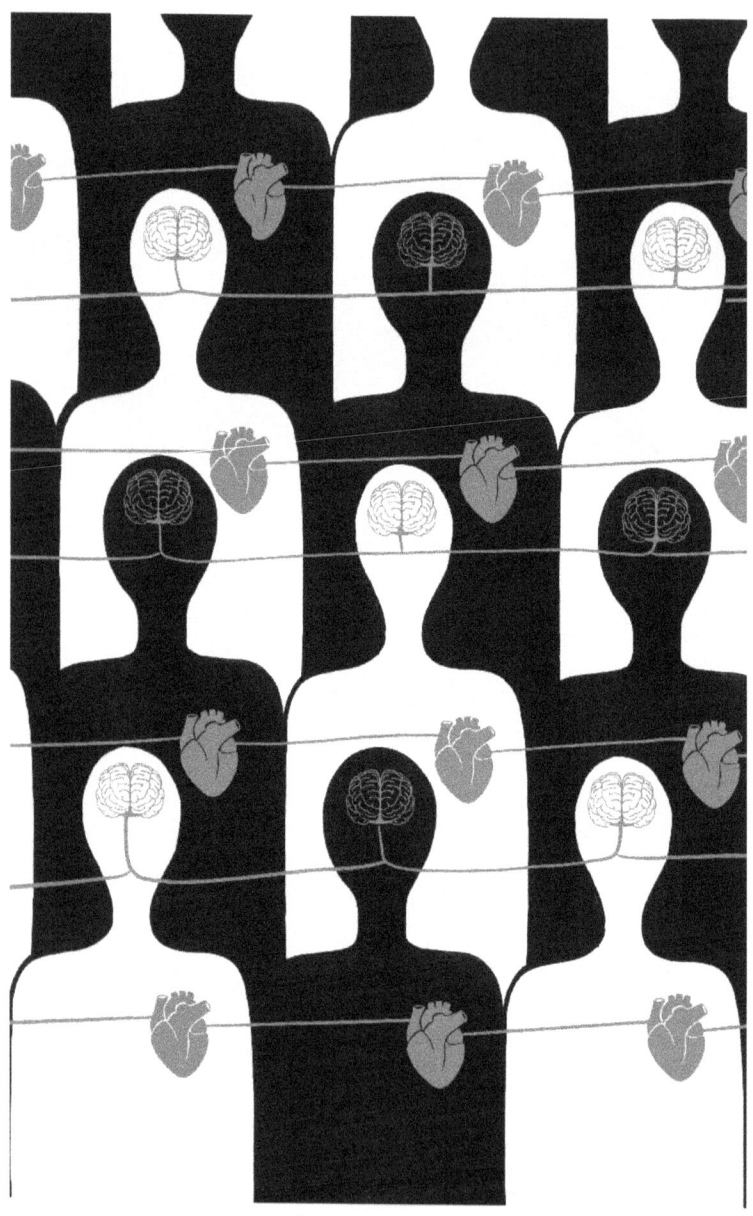

Mere Idiots

A fools play in a field,
Fighting amongst beliefs.
Only mere idiots believe it's a power
great enough to yield.
The power of filling the gap, there'll never be relief.
Eternal suffering is all you get.
Filled up the empty void, have you yet?

Believe in nothing to start believing,
Though acting sane when sinned.
Of all who are leaving,
Yet, afraid to admit the superiority has been killed?
Even better, he was never the ring leader.
He was just the lion in the hands of the players

MIMI

Bloom, Rise.

Dawn ascends after hellish bloodshed,
All the opened eyes avert theirs to the ones shut.
Perhaps the ones to breathe are lucky,
Yet, why does this burden seem so heavy?

Now, grab a hold of thy sword.
Swing ahead, not at thee but at shore.
The sun must shine upon contact your blade,
That is when the world acknowledges, you rise.

The night of terrors may vanish in brisk,
Must all the tragedies we faced, disperse in a blink?
There may never be an end as you seize to survive,
Yet that is why, you must fight for your side.

Monsoon is soon to come,
Sorrow fills up all the silence,
Perhaps emptiest roars made us realise,
Our lives would be nothing without violence.

The Vast Void

A solemn thought given once in a lifetime.
One that fills all knowledge, all clues, all the gaps.
The ever so complexity, curiosity dare feels like a crime.
If I dig deeper, what may I find?

A falling abyss is to give thy peace,
As long as it fills my void, to finally be at ease.
Open minds only assure emptiness.
Of the thoughts that fill my mind,
They are sure to be defined.

As the nights seem too long to think,
In the mornings, it feels like a pure frink.
The world seems to come next end,
All their voices in my head are starting to bend.

But as the sense hear the distortions form,
The mind goes numb, the body turns warm.
It's the thought itself which trapped thy curiosity,
Something to be washed in, for the rest of eternity.

MIMI

Froid Friend Puzzles
To Mirai,

The social circle widens at the drop of each being,
Though you were Kalon, did that circle catch your need?
Only certain puzzles fit the circle, and as much as you force them in,
There's always one piece that always has been.

There may be some pieces that stick in if we force them enough,
Yet, we'll never forget that hard piece which was rough.
Perhaps next time, instead of pushing the piece in,
We'll take our time to look beneath its skin.

To what lays more than the eyes perceive,
You never had to be the perfect puzzle piece.
The social would break eventually,
It must be rebuilt so why are you laughing so miserably?

The Sorrows of Humanity

It is as if a creature ever so clueless, building on stones.
Perhaps those stones were half crusted by our bones.
But as the deserted stare around for a while, avoid what clues give sensations.
As we seek what is called knowledge, each answer leads to new questions.

Maybe life could have been simpler, if we wanted it to have been.
Yet, as we all share the same blood as overall, the same skin, deep within.
It's rather the way we chose to solve what was ahead of us that mattered,
Our realities , it was for sure no souls would have scattered.

I'm okay with being lost for the rest of eternity,
But yet, I oath to never forget your harsh brutality.
The one you had to ponder upon for me,
Which you had dreamed about, for thee.

MIMI

Neutral Times

It is when we get locked in the idea of fasades,
That we lose sight of what we have that fades.
The advantages of great portrayals tricks the mind,
To rot the soul, something which may creep upon humankind.

When we look at time as nothing more than mere tocks,
It is then when it laughs and takes away thy dwelling clocks.
But when you view the world in colors nothing more neutral,
There is when the suffering is bleeding for internal.

Selfishness isn't something to be stopped,
It is something to be accepted and propped.
Not in the way of the higher,
In a way where it's so much, it shall no longer be dire.

MIMI

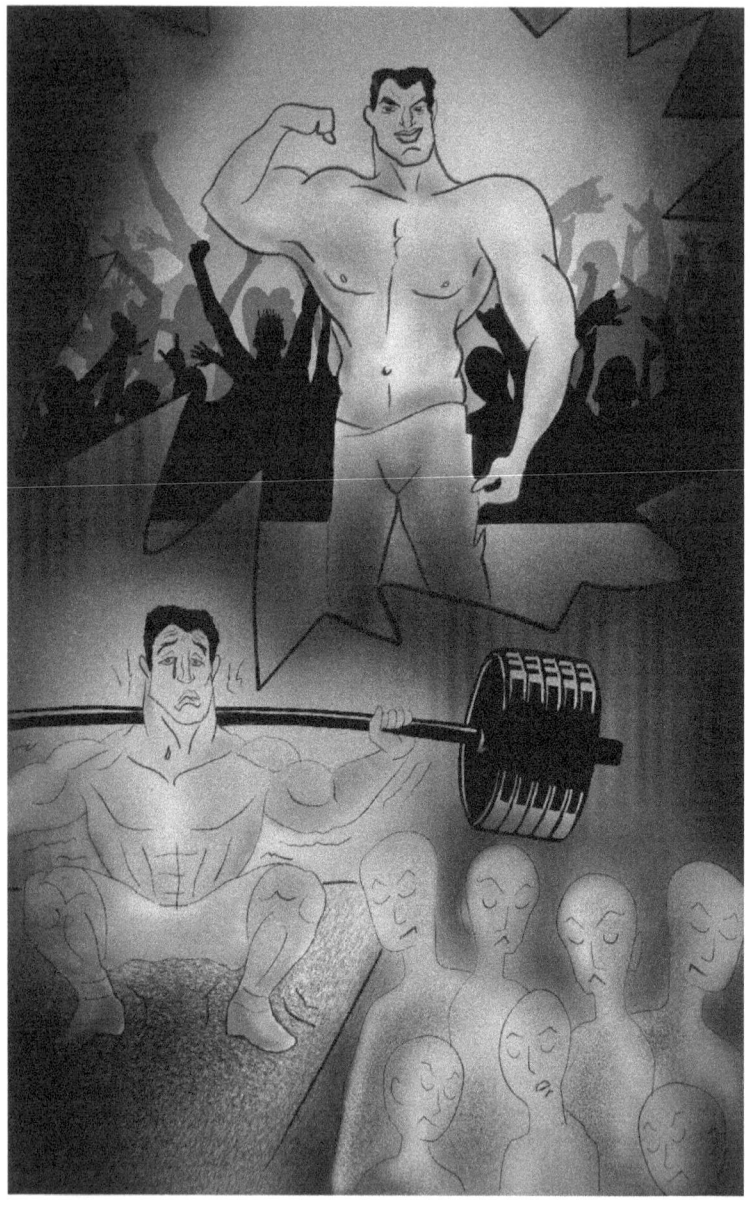

Deceptions Misheard

Each kind has their sorrows,
Yet it is the one with joy, that everyone follows.
But when we communicate of the unlikeliness of the mellow,
Why must all the people hide and act so shallow?

When thee whisper of thy tragedies,
The rest must laugh, their screams must be your agonies.
Falling from high, their advice becomes hypocrisy,
No one cares for prolonged melancholies.

They may say the minds mature and modern,
But they all know, the truth remains, it must harden.
So as our so-called advanced, though all my trues have been lanced.
I kept the secrets for thee, so next time your views must be enhanced.

The One-Way Sail

I have left my trail,
years and years, as I fade
To the world, I sail
it's a lovely crusade.
To succeed or to fail,
the man asks, "greater pain to trade?"
Just as wounded soars ahead, everywhere.

Fascinating tales I heard of the one-way sail,
Though most fear, there lie some who pother.
Stare at the stars above, a peaceful scare.
Wish to have been guided by another.
Merely a way to have been able to do it better.

I realise of no memories left behind
all that is, the hard work and pain
no joy or sorrow of lonely sparrows
thus, shut the eyes of the blinded Colours
and open those of a wider number
the vast purity of the impure
they believe of my fun journey,
out of this world.

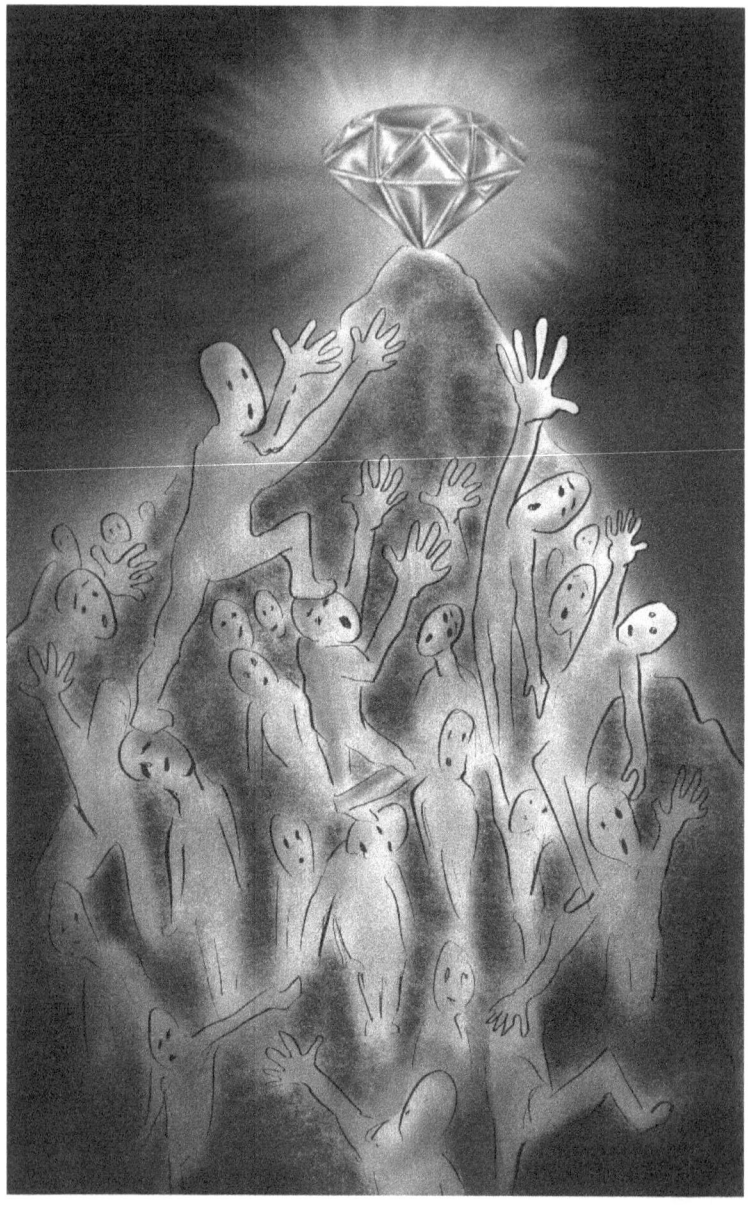

Righted Wrongs

They rage as if they were sane,
Scream as though you would never do the same.
The beliefs of the injustice makes the insides ramble,
Though if morals frustrate money, it too is up for a gamble.

Sincere judges of our own mishaps,
Mishaps leading to righted wrongs of disagreements.
As though the full truth must've been vagued, perhaps.
Must it be a curse or blessing to feel as though high,
When all we are, mere flecks of the same side.

If thy sins are meant to be atoned,
Must there be point of life, where all facts are condoned?
Though series of gaps leave intimate memories,
Of nothing to rely for, no longer souls to please.

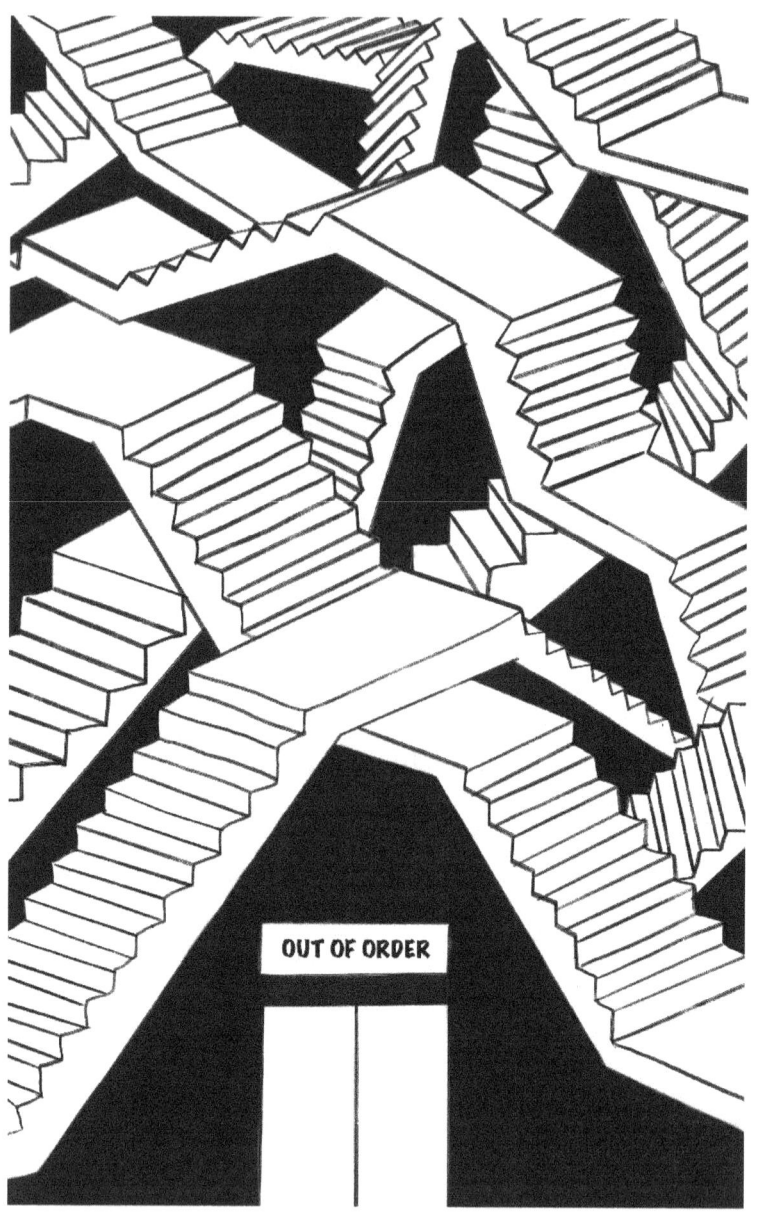

Elevator

The glance of joy at first sight,
Something to be sworn, oathed, achieved with all might.
Somewhere with all stairs, far heights.
Though there may be lots to climb, an elevator would have been nice.

The stairs have all kinds, with all types of finds.
Some were enormous, some were petite.
Most of them climbed so high, all with no seats.
The most frightening of all, if to fall, there were no tears left to bawl.

To fall back one step, take one to move ahead.
Shakes the spine, brings out all the hard times.
But though years and years to climb those stairs,
Perhaps an elevator, for a while, would have been fair.

Thee blossomed, I wilted.

They say not much, as it is easy to play.
But to stare at thyself and worry the world, starts the gloomiest day.
Try and try, A constant loop, forever in hell.
1 step ahead, 999 more steps to dwell.

Though it seems to start, hands to crush and feet be crumble,
It must have been simple, that is why the fear is to act humble.
Utter jealousy and rage to glance at the effortless of those,
As that moment looks long, all effort put in shatters, much shows.
Limbs break to feel,
To fall to end, pure defeat.
So as stare at the gifted, look at the reflection of gloom.
The will to toil, the hope to never again try to bloom.

The whole world must laugh at the try too hard,
Years to master, simple to call, caught in the facade.
Once more, itching my salted wounds as they dare ask me to try.
I shan't dare but look through all struggles, hoping thou find torment in my eyes.

Rusted Coins

Through endless means, paths and history I've watched to see.
The malicious thought of "money" left pondered questionably.
Endless fights, kills, and crimes asked why it was necessary.
Pleased perhaps, having the comfort of it letting it all be.

Must the others always be one step ahead? Though we expect the same.
Their delightful ways for most have me cower in shame.
Tis for who, soon for all to sink they may awaken to be shaken cold.
Because of all they had, yet cried out for more, more and more.

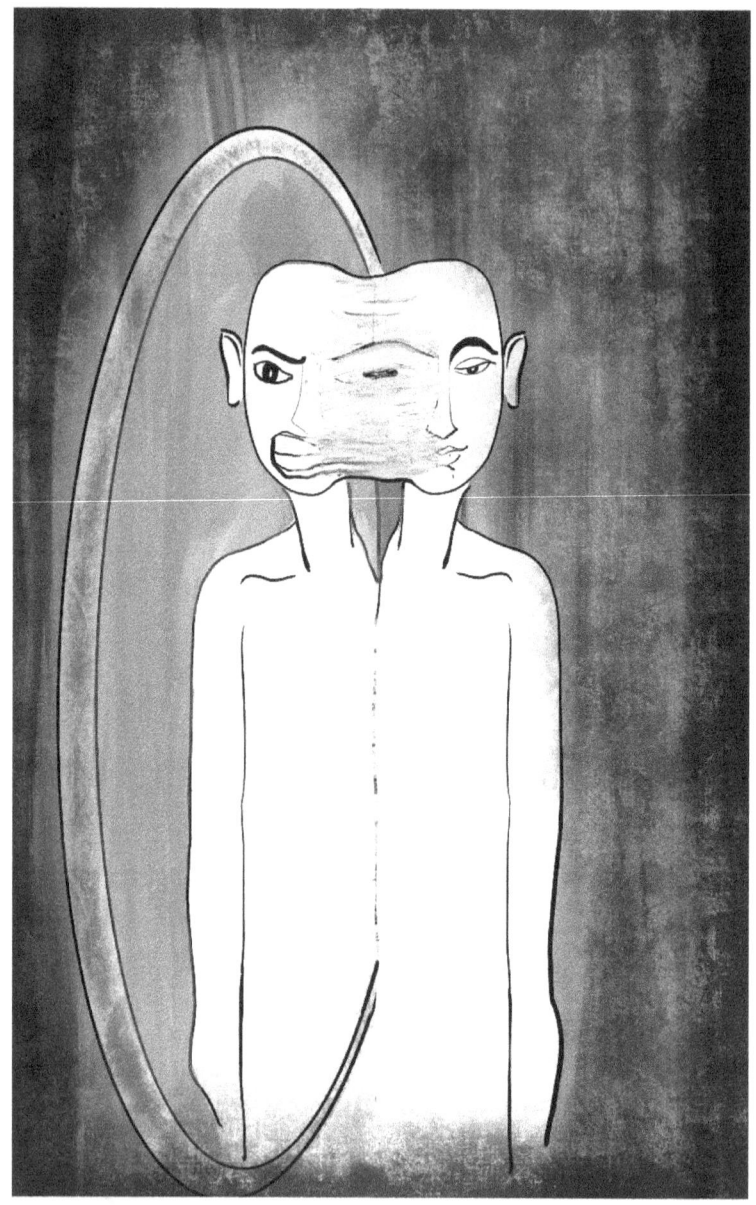

Reflection

I avoid to stare at the one who blankly mists to see,
Jitters run me down when asked how I feel.
When the answer lies vastly amongst the meets of stars.
Close enough to feel, Glimpses away of doubt left afar.
Absurdly must you speak of how and when you believe?
Painted images of idealists was your only last wave of relief.
Night o' hue, when caved in deeper to hidden trues of deceit.
Ponders upon question of: how miserably was peace hard enough to seek?
Was it far too evident, far along it was me who was thy eternal foe?
Standing behalf your shadows, far from twilight, where all atrocious creatures grow.
As I've sunk far deeper, farthest than all eyes can await to witness.
'Tis time to accept all nails stabbed against ever immoral me,
As Avoidance was never a possibility for the blinded allowed to see.

MIMI

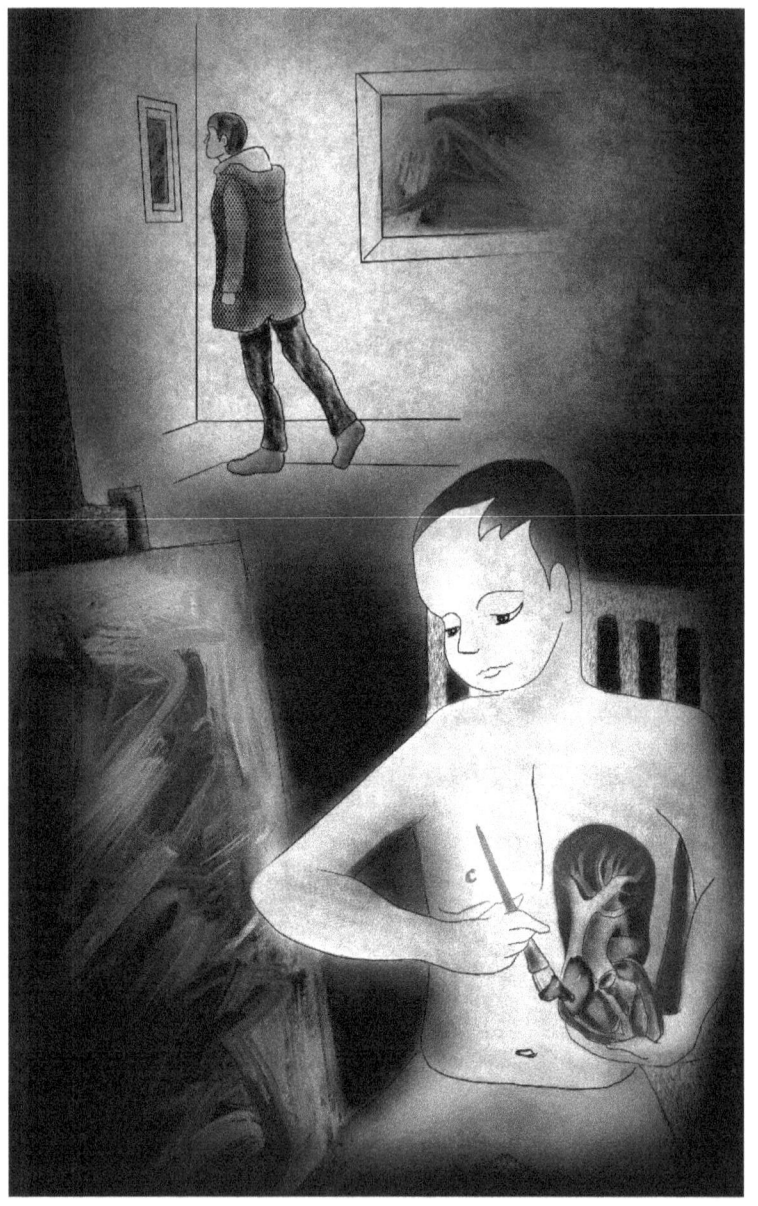

Magnum Opus

Struck at the worst or lightened by ease,
For most delightful sorrows are given to please.
When the most is to be laughing in feels.
Me crimson screams is for what is allowed the great deal.

Each masterpiece roamed me spiral bricked thoughts,
When was it the master never edged the sea to create such raving schemes.
'Twas thee admirer what the art pulled me out of drought.
Rain poured down drafting such darkness, my canvas absorbed them.

To pick up a thin felt pen, fill the paper with heavy says.
Was what me write, a letter for all to be burdened each day?
If carrying a thousand tales allowed me to have been left hollow.
Proved to leave me bury, when vengeance merely follows.

— *tragedies create great art*

Sight Sighing

Wails and cheers were given by those considered to be peers.
Descending to the depths of vile when all decided to slash ears.
Another day, another time, must it arrive to pit struck lethargy?
When I for sure, far left the warmth o' comfort to get all the praise.
Nor could I feel, touch, with numbness welded leeching of their greed.
The top of this mountain isn't quite the sight for what I wished to see,
In rock bottom all I ever got was no one's and everyone's apathy.
The waters no longer beholden my sights to the enchanted I fled.
Now was it when the crowd yielded me feet, as to show appreciation.
Clueless when I was to be treated higher, when my feet tied to a heavy dread.
Like a magnet, only attracted when I let them go, raced far too ahead.
The rock bottom allowed me ways to drift far off bitter hearty realisation.

End Cycle

For what spins along wheels of strain on vicious miles,
As though only rounds danced amongst me spinning the middle.
It captured my time, so it stays with me and never flies.
Meaning of what's hidden, such as the endless cycle dare not let me smile.

I no longer please to carry twice the burden for sheer superiority.
Over all humbleness, for the sour taste left behind of dread,
This cycle chased me, for fears of what remains are these miseries.
Churned far too long, to allow all promises to be made left dead.
The bypassers believed it abstract of such disarranged brain.
I shall repeat it 10,000 times if I shall to get rid of the cycle.
Though I know, uncertain it is to escape such a manipulation.
To have not started it all would have been better than this repetition?

Era's finest Knave

These years grew wings to soar like birds,
Fond memories of thee, I dare not ever heard.
Monsoon shan't arrive at the glimpse of thou,
As thou dishonest man made such vulnerable clouds.

Thou built your works, kept the jewels.
Rest the nobles all felt like fools.
Beliefs and morals felt mere possibilities,
To those left vague of empty realities.

How wicked must one be to cry like me,
me who blamed the ones I left no remorse nor glee.
Power left thou reigned for centuries: hear thy name,
Mustn't they know thy cunningness? Oh, what a shame!

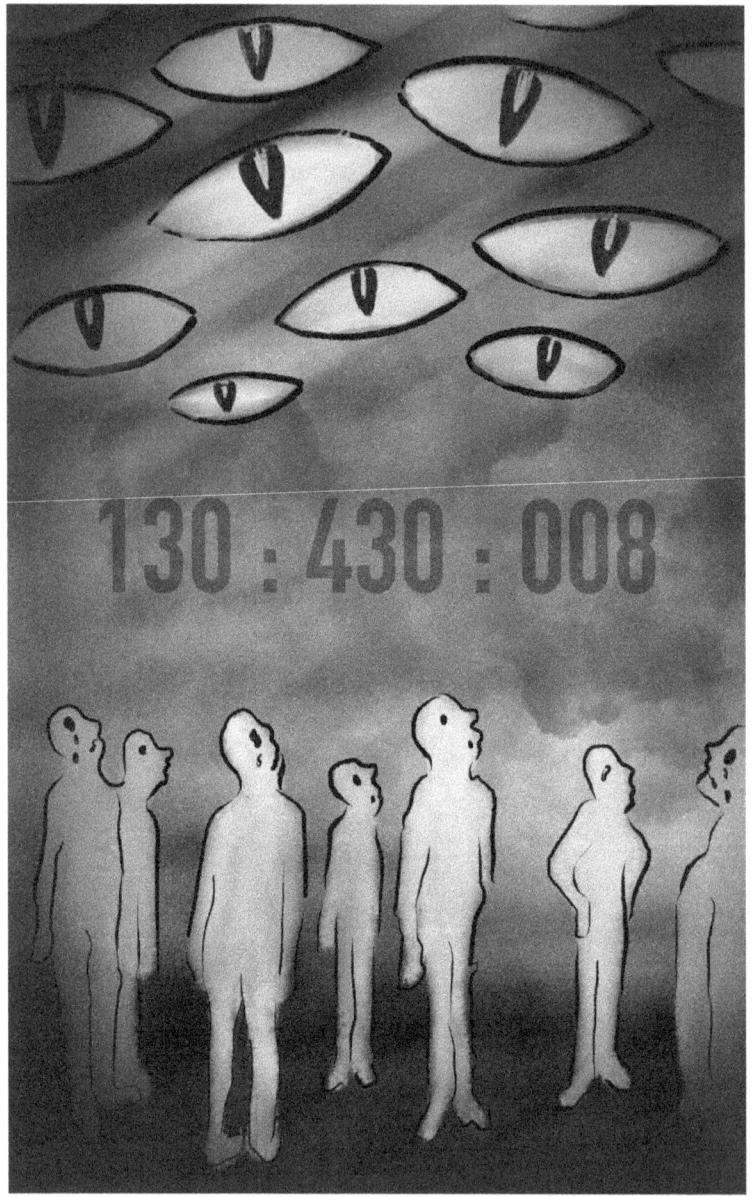

Man Made Malice

The infinities apart, the skies bond us all.
Man is known as God, yet it must be our downfall.
Must we say rationality behalf of emotions,
Inferior to all, we make God our devotion.
Man may be called superior,
Man may always be ulterior.
Yet as death is faced upon us,
We shall scream for mercy, make a fuss.

The rest must frown upon us,
Of our sins, shown for discuss.
If God has created man, he is great.
Yet as we struggle, it is no longer fate.
We say we believe, yet we contradict,
There may never be a thing small enough to constrict.
Utter greed captures love, though trust me as I say,
There is no such thing as a price to pay.

Wonder, curiosity, imagination kills all facts.
That is why man is afraid of death,
Perhaps it is because of our comfort of what we know,
Against all the things, the doubt of where we go.

MIMI

Yin and Yang

Look at the faces of those who strike to shine,
While I hide in my face deep shadows, for the free dime.
Hear the speaks of corrupt, their righted sins and wrongful rights.
Never the thought comes to mind if no balance free my spite.

To the lines that cracks all, the receives of all beliefs.
Gaining focus to the ones blurred for close intrigue.
Chances were few for disarray, yet never to be cruel.
Acceptance high agreement, thus, fate swore never true.

"Good" deems no great yet "bad" serves the demons.
Inner depths of why to prove who is correct, meaningless reasons.
For fulfilled years no one dares to utter the honest binds,
Perhaps it was because it goes further, to destroy the peculiar minds.

MIMI

Burdened Baggage

Picked up all the boxes left at me doorstep,
The fragile, the large, the small, the simple.
Pondered tightly on to me, never knew the
unloading left me miserable.
When no chance was given to escape today,
immense fears took over as I got out of bed.

Perhaps I was too old to be left young,
For as gloomy years lay far for as I can fly.
These boxes, wrapped on to me for years, were quite
burdensome.
Scraping away the boxes too allowed me explore the
rainy skies.

Guffawing lightly, yet enough the birds soar
through.
Averting sympathy to spewing squirrels left in blues.

MIMI

The Path In Between

'Tis time to part ways for far voyages,
Need not run, for when the woods require sighting along a tread.
As I turn for the other, fear held back the longing to cross ahead.
Thus, veiled sincerely, my path ties along the middle of no ends.

Must you tremble? As you have intended, life was mere.
Drenched of grudges past the path; for no end came soon.
For the vision to spear, they all innocently grip onto a knife.
So as far as they reach to stab my wounds, I shall too be sincere.

Ah! As I far see, they'd act with no remorse whisking ever so prudently.
Preach with the chins held up high, their throats allowed all projection of lies.

~~Hero~~ Villian's Arc

Rage me not, when said to have questioned loyalty was what I shred.
For as, the shards were not the ones thrown by me vicious head.
It was far too easy for the simplicity to rapidly evolve a smirk,
Is that when you must finally get on your knees when no remorse was left to search.

The skies painted blue not but eternally, close enough to fade dull.
When the skies turn red, for that the clouds dance in such elation.
Soon my wings freed me bones and scorns, as time was new for a revolution.
Was your vividness scavenged wrong? When me raised left you null.

Silently the east rivers swayed last night,
For all bodies passed along distorted was indeed a horrendous sight.
Yet their joys of scream never flawed as much, 'twas their fright.
For what could grab a caged creature lost in the weakest daze,
The soul must ascended above all emptious flares.

MIMI

Woesome Witch

There once lived a lady drifting over the British sail.
Hereby her arrive, the whole town followed to hear her marvellous tale.
Left beholden by controversies, doubt and despair.
To have voiced their thoughts like her, not a single one dared.

Each night flew the British sails, taking away their reproachful witch.
Dawn raced far soon, standing at fire to be beheaded.
The journeys and mysteries were soon taken away by a lone myth.
Villagers of empty stomachs and empty heads, oh how their creativity descends!

Years pass by as no sound left the mouths of the miserable beings.
Neither tunes, rhymes, nor resonance set a bliss for the lethargic.
Fairies and angels sparked the delicacy, yet came the witch along her ravish meanings.
Necessity, as end it was for creativity shares parts to fade, sorefully tragic.

After Death, no life ahead

Simplicity I felt, when I was knocked on the door.
Inquired; Pessimist, sceptic, Nihilist, and farther more.
"Clueless" whispered back when asked what I felt.
For sure, existence for me had no reason left.

Deep in the waves they left me buried,
When I had asked thee to bury me sunny.
Oh, how I recall such memories of us merry,
Still the voices held on my shoulders way too heavy.

Neither did I want to have flown far from thee.
Yet, when their ears shut, the world trapped me in blues.
The ease at the moment was when I believed to be free.
When shall I smile back, till now I have none of the clues.

Perhaps optimist, believing, or happiness too.
Lift me off the crimes they yelled at me for.
Now, you mustn't cry as it isn't as cruel,
I am now flying, Now of that I am sure.

Haunted House

Finally came the time, I took one step on the ruins of me heartfelt house.
Sharp rays stung me down on my knees.
The sight to lay my eyes upon were merely the shards of emptiness' mound.
For sure, this certainly is not the house of what I bleed.

Words that repeat on my dwelled head have lost all simplest meaning.
Yearning to sounds followed by whispers of who shattered my house.
That awoken with grim purposefully leaving all the maids mourning.
Such fragments of glass scratched their perceived eyes, now came the realisation of such a wistful house.

As far as I lived, the neighbourhood was stunned, far too perplexed.
No sounds left my beloved house when doorbells rashed in.
Up till spring, I too never sensed such rest.
Comfort of the house I linger around was far too lean.

Now thou invited me to ask of what it meant for such a useless house.
For when joy I seek certainly never lied in such oblivious sympathy.
Yet, warmth hid close to me in a heartfelt, now bloodred house.
When I chose for once joy, I no longer hear to wail in agony.

MIMI

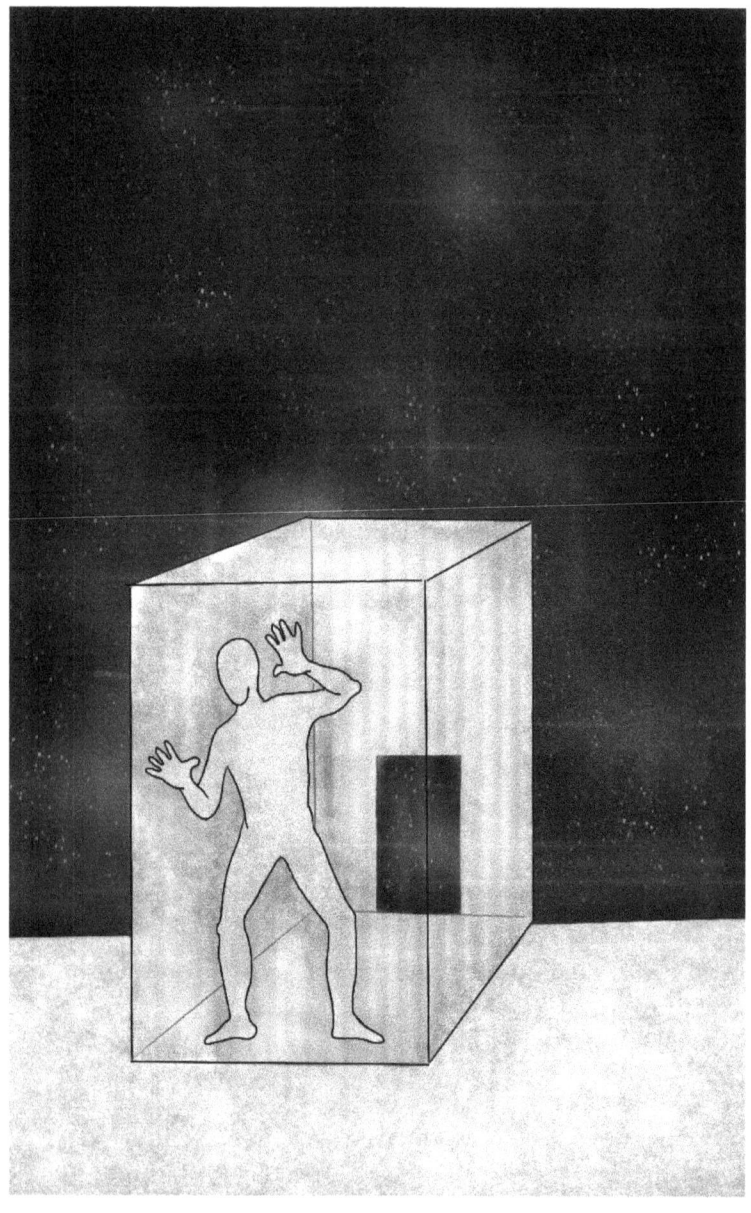

Endless Infinity

These senses have yet grasped hold of my spine.
When I observe spinning all around me.
I shan't see this reality be ever so fine.
Whereas time past, future lies, and all are free.

Why must they limit their vision to all that is seen?
Tis' the widest, possible line humanity ever reached.
Mysterious it may be, yet why tilt your heads far beyond,
When life itself to explore for us has just begun.

Pondering to associate meanings with actions left to display.
Who ever chose to hide what lies beyond what is there to say?
Abstract may it be, yet breach it beneath the skin to allow comfort.
Of the words I say, that allows your curiosity to never enter slumber.

Write I will, as words displayed my thoughts sincerely.
As my reveries of the endless allows me to gain perspective,
Sudden realisation hit me of us living too merely.
Despite it all, how foolish was I, remaining frantic

Lacuna

I've lived quite long to experience some of all,
As I've heard talks of what feelings belittles their soul.
Pain, loneliness, rage, jealousy, or fear that makes them crawl.
With the heart to breathe, the numbness to be felt is the worst for sure.

To have not been high or low, loud or quiet, guilty or joyous.
The emptiness of the numbness makes me question what I seek.
Day and night, try to gain a smile to tune or sorrow for turmoil.
I'd much rather feel anything than nothing trapping me in deep.

Bleed I must if I have to, sing a song if I lie there in solitude.
How I wish, something reigned over this hell, all so soon.
So I wonder if this numbness be following me after my years,
Laugh I will, cry I will, out loud so the numbness never reaches my fears.

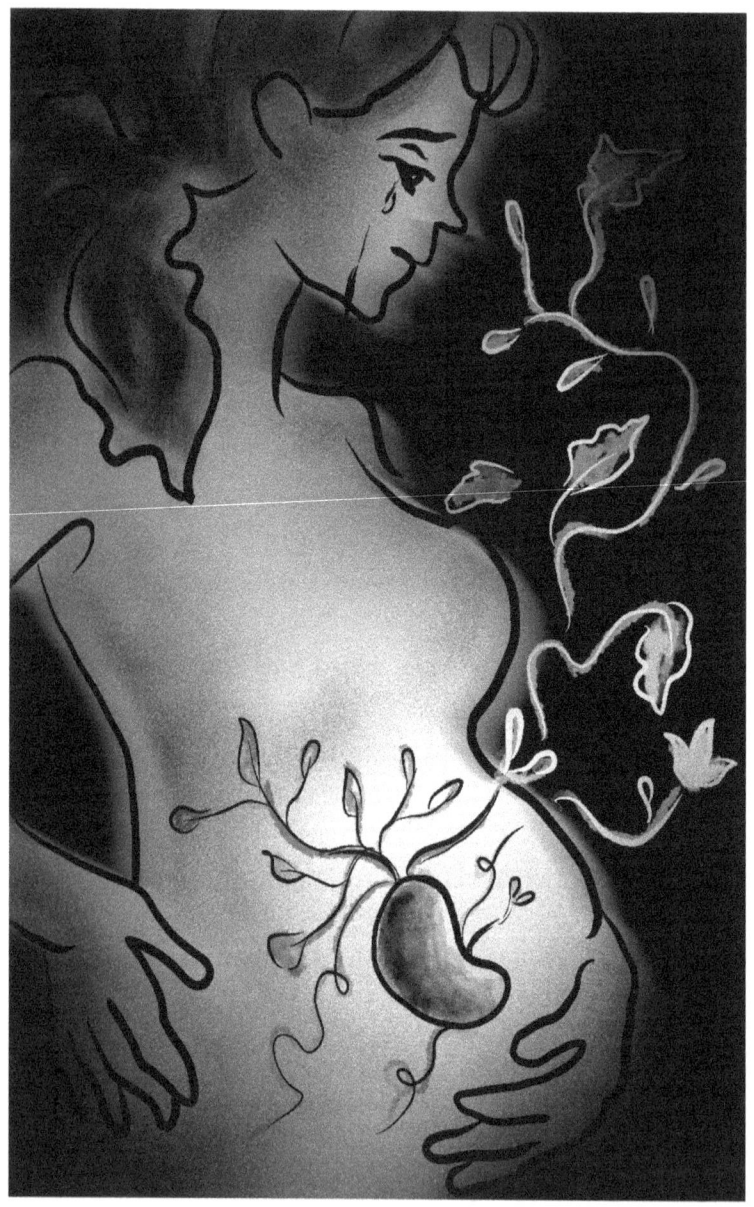

W Women, L 1964

They push out life, you'll push out turds.
Yet why is it, I am treated upon your words.
I am not but a mere arguer, I only arrive to state thou facts.
To harm those who birth, pray to the who you hurt?

The gift of giving life is by the woman,
The woman taken for granted.
She who must struggle upon her own,
Yet, why is she looked down on the most?

Was it because you were afraid?
Afraid of being overtaken by a mere woman?
That's why you'll be superior, in the depths of your heart,
You fear the greatest, the chosen, the true piece of art.

Time Turns to Trees

Must I write of what society enjoys to see?
Am I solemn entertainment for a while, for thee?
So as the time turns to trees,
Tis' true, I have millions of thoughts to seize.

Though life comes and goes, it is records that stay.
Though the body may die, the soul and mind never decay.
Years and years of experiences piled up in a stack all for you,
So take thy time, look around, as I have experience to add, for the new.

Now the time turns to trees,
Beneath my feet, it looks as though I have been set free.

The tree; The Witness

Don't act as if you know what happens behind the large stone walls.
Because a tree grown in shadows or a tree grown in sun,
Is the same for all of you.
Don't come to me with your insincere values or morals.
Because the only landscape anyone sees,
Is always the trees with the beautiful leaves.

Is it because of your persona that you are this gentle?
If you had a choice, what would you do if life was existential?
You give no care to the flowers unbothered,
For you, it's all about if or if not I'm sobered.

All you give voice to is the flower which blossoms most,
Yet, why mustn't you water the other ones, as if I'm just a ghost.
As you sit in peace to relay for your other,
Never dare to think of me as you are just that of another.

Obscure for sight

The wordless desperation for the cheers led not by you,
Must it be sad to feel the need to lone yourself, avoiding every blue.
Silence soars for the thoughts to darken and engage,
My empty bedroom no longer seems faced as the escape.

Their faces seem like pure disturbance to genuine peace,
As to gain the urge to rip off each head, though, the veins screech.
Not of rage, furiousness, or anything glimpsing into riptide,
Just of the sadistic life to have been said followed was an ugly ride.

While the sting of pain follows each curve insight,
What I write may never follow appreciative light.
Tis me screams with ache for those soon to arrive,
This heartfelt letter was a new start, not a goodbye.

MIMI

The solitary man

Sits an office surrounded by those,
All those who work with no repose.
It may seem as mediocre as raises mantle,
But with them all leading the same lives, is it just coincidental?

He comes home each night, the same time.
Goes to bed just at 11, that way he could see his stocks tomorrow at 7.
Though the circle repeats, on and over, one where he could never leave.
He is a solitary man, success was way far before any eternal peace.

Though he may seem as a man in vain,
There's quite a few who too share his pain.
It's the lies put to show the true corrupt,
You can deny it but, in this circle, changes are never abrupt.

Pawn

One or two, thou sacrifice all for who?
Futile shield, to have more solitude, their eyes see just a value of few.
Would thou awaken from the position, stand to see from the player's view?
To have moved all steps ahead, no cross behead, sure to align in tune.

Rightly may be the king's game as feeble queen's vain.
Of to stare at two of unfrightly, still allow the knight to be let?
If captured though, thy feelings and bleeding dare not let the game end.
As all the pieces let alone their lives, the king turns red to see his pawns and their delts.

'Twas useless, the king's value left sacrificing over the black and white board.
He dare not have seen the misery left on the knocked out empty pons.
At last though, ponder upon the questions which swallow them up whole,
If there was any use for their sacrifice, loss, to show if their deaths were wrong.

Far-fetched Forest

Mere joy from short lasting peace,
For eternal journeys, through rocks instead.
Is it wrong to ever have euphoria, from the strain to feel?
Though knowing the sun on the left, it was easy to choose the thorns ahead.

Just how the sweetest savouries leave the biggest cavities,
Bitter tasting flowers medicine oft lift ideas along means to flee.
The first bite tilts the mollys whilst the last leaves the poisoned lilies.
For all steps have been taken over me, flocks have cut the thorns, really!

For those thorns that give roses, rash silence no longer closes.
If for blissful moments to strive, it is now the path of where to die.
Young to feel, old for free, this journey is not what expects for me.
To look at another, living lushful in the feather, hide the need to scream.

MIMI

Mundane

For what it was to fall over on sharp needles,
Miles went on searches of reasons to ever resonate
Thou finally opened thy eyes to the world so atrocious
But who sits on the grass field dreaming of weeping on a bed of roses?

Leaves may fall at time of autumn to race close near,
For sure their brisk meets of ends shreds in crystal clear.
Now when was the last time to ever have to write of sheer spring?
When all these thoughts, mists, and clues still have me tingling.

Winter around the corner, the place of comfort freezes soon ideas.
How could one ask to gather round to smile at one another?
When I must be sitting in misery, clueless of clouds racing further.
Would the fire light bright if the mind would rest for moments,
Where winds howl, rains streak, and all flowers wilt the purest.

Quest of Time

The time has come, tocks of gold!
'Tis arrived neither too soon nor too fast.
Thou mildly waited, empty in the cold.
Thy mind reserved always for the future or past.
As thou do not regain memories of now.

The time has come, thou behold!
brushed on thy shoulder leaving thou cold.
When shall it leave? Thou keep wondering.
The past, present, future, all in pondering.

The time shall not wait, grasp ahold!
Thou recall the old self who proclaimed that thee,
Shan't wonder when, thee see the time unfold.
The present it is, how could thou dream to flee?
All that lies ahead of thee yet thou cannot see.

Yet, when the time has come it'll ring the bell.
Thou still awake recall and reminiscing of how it could be,
When it lay there, amongst where thou hid to dwell.
Why not let the burden away to let thou finally be free?
The time has left, leaving thou in the cold.

People Pleaser

The new chapter of the story starts to be prevailed,
One where I awakened of the bane hidden from me.
Far too long I was blinded to allow myself to see,
No matter how warm, how hard my care sheltered,
A lot more they expect ; as all my efforts go uncared.

Trembling inside of the miseries they may perceive,
Bury the truth of myself far than they'll ever try to reach.
As one concerns, worries, and fears only of what others are,
In circles I go, endlessly never being able to get away or far.

Handed all the pieces they ever asked or wanted from me,
And handed it I did, and far beyond they ever wondered of.
More and more, they all acted unbothered, careless and free.
When and why did I ever dare try to please them far too long?
As though, a puppet hung by a string of mere empty means

I like being Young

The fresh scent of a breezy morning's youth.
Such a fragile, naive, and warm heart, mind and soul.
The start of exploration which makes one sole.
Such feelings of heart ache, rush, and feelings crushed.
There may never come days again, I'll feel that shame.
The true savoury of youth, as blossoming of flowers.
The bud arises, A time to learn, forgive, forget and live.
Friends, lovers, family. Sparks with all of them in between.
I would never like to let go this feeling of warmth, my youth.
I'd relieve the stress, save it for perhaps another day or year.
shed tears of the things I believed worse at the hard times.
dense and shallow were the problems, as they were seen.
A long life I had ahead of me, why would I have anything to fear?
The Colors so vibrant to my eyes, I'll never allow them take my dream.

MIMI

POETRY EXPLICATION

Mere Idiots

The poem is about: Discrimination against beliefs. In society, how one can be discriminated against strongly as to believing in one thing over the other. As though they all have no answers, no ways, only their foolishness and superiority can be used as their strongest weapon. Sometimes, they deny the facts over their pride which leads to superiority amongst all. In the end though, they all act as fools to ask for salvation. The meanings vanish, it's all the same in the end. All their acts, words, thoughts of superiority, discrimination, in fights. They're mere idiots.

Bloom, Rise

The poem is about: The end of war. One side left victorious, the other left dead and defeated. Yet this win was not victorious, rather blood-filled guilt. The reason didn't seem as big to steal all their lives, to see the by-passers left in tears. To pick up the sword handed to you showing that you were the chosen, when indeed the sword was used to slay the heads of many. When the sword swung ahead at them all, that is when it was that we rose? To the victories which far left burdens. Yet, war is the only way to just admit the wrong, is it not? That is why, the flowers of the next era must be watered whole heartedly to bloom, to rise.

The Vast Void

The poem is about the vastness of nothing. The depths of how far each individual could ever reach with asking many questions, how one's mind can grasp onto ideas and the abstract. How sophisticated life is to have been caged to a simple mindset, yet in a closed mind the thoughts you yourself can deny or develop. Also about a thought, the only lightbulb thought that when given once in a lifetime, it is something that you still question up to years. No leads, no clues, nothing. All their ideas, perspectives, only make your head empty as to why they're right, you're wrong. Yet the fear of what may be discovered may leave you in horrendous shock. It is the vastness of the void, the nothing that gives us peace. The vast void.

Froid Friend Puzzles

A poem written based off of an observation I made on a specific friend. As time went by, I realised it wasn't just her struggling with this. There's far too many people struggling with this and personally, I too indeed have. An odd puzzle piece. The one that can fit in a spot perfectly but it isn't the right piece, it's shaped so oddly yet it can fit in most places. Just like that, there are some people who try to shape themselves to be someone they're not when they believe they too have a place just right for them, they believe there are places which aren't better for them but as long as they're surrounded with the other pieces of the puzzle, it's comfortable enough to not be the perfect puzzle piece.

The Sorrows Of Humanity

The poem is about : Building a high society from all the knowledge of before. There was a point with doubt, If indeed all that was being visualised, shown, sensed was true or just motionless dreams. To be so clueless, so curious, to have discovered all that is undiscovered. The weight of carrying all and beyond, to discover deeper in the shallow waters. As the world keeps progressing, developing, and advancing.. wouldn't the meaning of curiosity and learning itself vanish? We want to discover as much as possible in our lives and pass it on to the rest, make theories for the future generations to prove, and also try to find the answer to it all. But deep inside, what if we try to avoid finding this answer of existence because it makes us lose all meaning of why we exist. Working on a dream, trying to reach the high point, all till death. This is indeed, the sorrows of humanity.

Neutral Times

Sometimes in life, we're trapped in facades. Rich, poor, smart, dumb. All of them are labels that attach themselves onto us. When we get caught onto the facade of higher, superior, greater, and smarter. This poem was about the facade of thinking that you are superior and great. That facade that gets you thinking that each step backwards is downfall. We get greedy, jealous, and selfish for more and more of the facade that we lose ourselves in the process to become someone who appreciates highly. Even in a colourful scene, it's still grey and dull for them because they believe there are prettier Colors. There is too much suffering in trying to be the higher person that when they refuse to take a step backwards, they get pushed back far too much in the end. Sometimes I wonder as well, if we give someone everything and more than they ask, at what limit will they get sickened of it all and decide to return to the neutral times?

Deceptions Misheard

This poem is about the way humanity is opened up and advanced to modern thoughts and beliefs. It's how we follow those with a bright future. Our role models always remain to smile, cheer us up, and care for us. Yet, most times when we hear of controversial or personal backgrounds of those role models, most start to perceive them differently. Perhaps it's because of the idealization we project onto that being, every move they do is being followed. This too follows the modern advanced mind, as much it shows that we support, believe, and love. When it reaches our deep core to make us insecure, they'll all turn their backs against who they once viewed highly, it was the unfairness of the deceptions misheard.

The One-Way Sail

A poem quite frankly considered fiction. If death was a journey, if life after it existed, It could be viewed as a sail. A one way sail. Perhaps no one who gets on the one way sail is allowed to return, or after they've seen what lies ahead, they don't want to return. On the sail though, lies a man, the journey man. He asks of your life well lived, pain it was for most as they regret. Here on the one way sail, you lie rested in peace for the whole journey. Shutting your eyes, memories can return as to how you lived your life. The ups, downs, and the in between. You could have lived far better, or you lived just right. Yet, guilt still remains. No one guided those who got on the one-way sail, no one gave any advice as to how to do it perfectly. If only there was a manual on how the one way sail functioned, those who get on the ship sail far away, as those left behind wonder of the journey that lies ahead. Empty it is, chaotic it is, you must get on to find out, the one-way sail.

Righted Wrongs

To take sides, let it be a fight, or any situation. We take sides of one believing they're better than the other. If one was to get angry at the wrongs of anything, if they were placed in the same situation, would most of them do the right thing too? It is just the simplistic view of the 3rd person which projects so much hatred on the wrong. In this poem, I wanted to write of how confusing people can be with switching up sides so fast. Establishing laws and rules of society to create a better community, we are indeed the judges of our own mishaps here to hate the wrong. This isn't mercy for the wrong, but a question. If bad or wrong was to disappear, would there be any meaning to righteousness? If society was led on by rationality rather than feelings, would there ever be a point to make? Isn't that why it is necessary for righted wrongs?

Elevator

This poem was inspired by the famous saying "To achieve greatness, take small steps, not big ones. Working hard as it's not a destination, but a journey". It's fascinating to see it projected onto the real world, though. It starts off with a passion, or driven thought. Then, it's as though we're automatically at the start of climbing stairs to reach milestones for finally achieving our dreams. It's frightening though, how small these stairs are yet how endless they are. Perhaps this was the reason they said not to take the large steps, it was easier to trip back and fall too easily. With all the hard work put in , all the blood, sweat and tears. A place with endless stairs for each person because it's said as a journey, a simple thought of what would happen if there was an elevator. Would it be more efficient or would it make the stairs useless? If life gets more and more efficient, so do our passions and goals to achieve, is there any true meaning to any of it at all?

Thee blossomed, I wilted.

A poem heartfeltly written as someone who felt that talent beat hard work. Those who watch from afar always see it as simpler once you're believed to be "good". Just merely work harder for half your life, try so hard till your limbs start to become weak. Suddenly arrives someone much better than you, they didn't even try to work as hard as you did. Easy it was, they made it seem as though all this was simple play. There vanishes, miles and miles of hard work soared through, crushed in seconds. Even trying to overcome it by trying to climb harder and quicker, they're always skipping ahead. Hell it is, perish you can when admitting how little you feel, how useless to feel. Giving up was rather a better choice than to see yourself defeated by a farther better person. Seeing all the love and passion you put in wilt, as you allow the other to blossom.

Rusted Coins

Money is highly valuable, everyone knows that. Society relies on money to a point where some are willing to leave their morals for the sheets of paper controlling their life. I observed to see what people did for money. Giving up on the things you like, making sacrifices, lying, cheating. This is the way of society though, the more money you get, the more you cry for more. Social status based on money, value based on money, justice based on money. I wonder if it's money that leads to dystopia or what we believe a fair equal society.

Reflection

Every person who exists cannot always be nice. No matter what you do or believe, everyone cannot always be a good person. As you can be a good citizen yet perhaps not a good father or sister. Whatever it may be, we live off balance. The most highly idealised people as well weren't always kind, "bad" is something which is needed to grow and develop. To see the true meaning of good itself. Every one of us is a reflection of ourselves. We could be the kind one perhaps or the average person society made us be. Yet, the reflection sometimes calls out to us. It hides darkly near us, waiting. Slowly, calmly waiting in the shadows of the shining person showed to be in joy. It is just if people choose to give control to such thoughts which make them good or bad. You can never get rid of it though, even if you choose not to live by it or listen to it. It was attached to you, it is partly what makes us human, our reflection.

Magnum Opus

Motivation driven by passion can be beautiful but I've questioned which is greater. Art made with passion or art made with sorrow. Every individual can share pain between one another and sure they can share joy as well. I choose to believe that art made with tragedy is more resonated with me as the feelings can be felt on a deeper level. Each person who strives for their grand work to ever be displayed; they work towards it. Your greatest work can be finished but what comes after? I wrote this from the perspective of anyone who ever produces work or any art. Some work for joy, some work driven by pain, and some work to be appreciated because it is those who appreciate the work that makes our work meaningful. It's the work we did most heartfelt, not passion, pain or sorrow. But the one we gathered every single thing we wanted to put down, want it to be seen in every perspective, appreciated or degraded, a mix of emotions created throughout the process. The last stanza was a personal one of my works. I do indeed know that it isn't the lightest or happiest topic to write about, it isn't the kindest either. Yet, I wrote with a mix of emotions, wrote everything I wanted to say, I was neither driven by passion nor pain. I just wrote since it came to me easily and I enjoyed it. This could perhaps be my magnum opus.

Sight Seeing

People only give appreciation to the great. That isn't wrong, but it's frustrating. Personally, for me I find it frustrating and raging. You must hit rock bottom in order to jump to the highest mountain, I had been taught that. Yet, I found comfort in the rock bottom instead of the top of the hill. When I was at rock bottom, no one dared to glance or ever think of me. I was alone, I enjoyed that loneliness though. It helped me know what was indeed permanent and what was temporary. I took my time to climb, even blinded by the thoughts or opinions by the people who never dared to speak to me on the rock bottom. Climbed, swam, raced to the top. Once I reached the top though, I despised those who started to then choose to open their eyes. Now mean to treat me great, superior, and better. They choose to talk to me and advise me, I wondered where all that went in the rock bottom. The hill was much more unsteady than the rock bottom. People at the bottom, ready to catch you if someone pushes you off. They'll praise you either way since you're at the hill. The rock bottom though, it has a sturdy ground. It'll remain and let you stay there a while or climb higher. That is why the sight there is far better than the sight up at the top.

End Cycle

I'm not sure what went through my head while

writing this poem as it was a series of things. Life felt like an endless cycle, a repeated cycle. Wake up, do the same routine, sleep, repeat. Endless and endless, walking on and on in this cycle. Sometimes carrying or doing different things to get rid of the cycle, or going on with the cycle till the day I die. It had a sour taste, extremely sour. Sour because it was repeated various times. The poem is also based on the quote "do it 10,000 times to reach perfection." I wondered if that would let me get rid of the cycle at least, allow me to see the end. There would always be new standards to fulfill so the cycle goes on. I wish to once at least reach the end of the cycle.

Era's finest Knave

This was a historical poem. I know I haven't witnessed history but I've read of it. I've read enough history on enough great, grand, historical figures and icons. I've read their stories as well. There are some selfish, cruel, brutal monarchs. I wanted to write this in the view of the people. We learn of these important monarchs and their vicious ways of reigning, I wanted to just make a perspective poem of it based on the people's views.

Man Made Malice

This is a poem of humanity as a whole. Our malice and lies we've displayed as a species. We act like we are superior, but when we know we've sinned, we lay down and pray for mercy. Is that superiority? Moments before dying, doesn't one feel fearful and inferior? If things are on our side, we'll start to appreciate it. If not, there perhaps isn't any meaning to be seen. I also see our beliefs as contradictory and confusing. If there's a line drawn for one to be forgiven or punished? There's too many questions. Yet I do know that greed mostly captures love. If you shred all the layers we have for being human, isn't it greed that allows us to call ourselves human? In the 3rd stanza, I wanted to question why exactly we're afraid of the term "death". Is it because of our imagination of what'll happen next? The idea of Heaven and hell, the afterlife? No one does know, it's a mystery. Something that's hard to solve, difficult, and complex, perhaps that's why we fear it. Fear of not knowing what happens next. All of this combined, everything we've strived for. We exist, create our own problems, some solve them and some destroy, we create beliefs or follow beliefs to showcase what and who is labelled. It's a man made malice, what we've created.

Yin and Yang

This poem is an add on to the other poem "righted wrongs". It's an in-depth edition as well. I was taught that "yin and Yang" stands for balance. Without darkness, light ceases to exist. Yet we strive for a world with no crime or wars. It's awfully confusing of a message that we're living in. It's as though we've adjusted to this normal. There's a fine line between good and bad and by just being good, you're not anything special but the second you're slightly bad, they'll all frown upon you. In my class, we were collectively asked a question if we would be "ignorant and happy" or "sad and aware". Quite many sided with the ignorant and happy and some too sided with sad and aware. A girl claimed that she would prefer to remain ignorant as the matter didn't bother her so why be gloomy? Another boy defended back saying that being sad and aware allows you to know what's going on around us, it allows us to find a way to develop and find the problem. Strangely, I remained in the middle. Both their arguments were fair, they had points and arguments. Is there a right answer to the question, though? Is there ever a right question when morals come into our rights? Isn't that why yin and Yang exists, to not make one superior and one inferior but to accept the darkness along with the light. To accept both sides as a whole, to be balanced and in between, then I understood the true meaning of yin and Yang.

Burdened Baggage

This is a poem I wrote when I realised I was 13. I knew I turned 13 on my birthday but it felt like I was 13 and was a teenager right at that moment. I was now a teenager, I had responsibilities and expectations on my back from all my family members, friends, etc. It was like a load of boxes of various things left at my doorstep. It was like the minute I was now "old", they never gave me time to settle down. Overwhelmed with the future's burden on me was misery. Though, these expectations, hopes, burdens are what I still carry up to this day. Sometimes though, they get quite heavy to carry but I have no time to be left young, it's overwhelming to act old now. As a child, I thought it was fun to have been left free too, being a teenager or being old. It was like being a bird, being free. But looking at it now, I wished I had remained young like a squirrel still seeking comfort in its tree.

The Path In Between

I heard the quote before that humans are neither good nor bad. They are in between. This poem was inspired by that quote. You cannot always be bad nor can you always be good. Your path that you take in life too , I believe can't always be good or always bad. There's no need to run in the path in between though, slightly walking is alright. Taking both sides of the path is alright, it doesn't make you labelled as bad or good. I'm still clueless as to whether all people start off innocent in the path in between and choose which path to get on. They fear the decision of which path they choose to be life changing. They all stand with the fact that their path should be the one to choose, the one which will lead to greatness. Each individual who built their own path and told people to walk through it. I just questioned how it would be to walk in the path between all of them. Even with their lies, truths, preaches, etc. If I remain sincere to my morals, just walking their paths and ways. What would change?

Hero Villian's Arc

I wrote this poem in a sense of one ascending. One awakening from the chaos they've been in for far too long. Not everyone in the world can be heroes, some must be villains. The person here had awakened in the heroic sense, yet were treated in a villianish way. The person chose to wake up from being silenced, questioned, and remaining naive. It enraged the world and questioned the person's loyalty when by far, it was the world that needed to question its own rules. A society that trapped everyone like caged creatures, telling them that doing this would lead to all sorts of grim or misery. The person chose to rebel and not listen to the norms of society, they chose to ascend.

Woesome Witch

I wanted to write this about the olden times and how society used to take in their beliefs and ideas that were given in various perspectives. There was only appreciation when it was sweet to their taste buds. To defy them, it would make you a witch or devil. I wanted to create a character who broke the norms of such a society, risking their life to tell their interesting perspectives and tales to those. The higher ups despised that though, as it was a different view from theirs. There onwards, they banished the so-called witch. I made this an in real life example which I witnessed a couple times. It didn't matter if I was right or if people were happy ,if it defied those with more power, I'd be condoned as someone terrible. Is it because they're scared? Jealous? Or their pride makes them far too egoistic.

After Death, no life ahead

I dedicated this poem to the people close to me, it was like a letter. I wanted to relate this to those too who ever tried to take their life away. It's when life is meaningless and has no value to you when you start to question things. Yet, it's as though you're free now but at the same time trapped in the voices of your head. I have far too many questions to ask those who ever took their lives away. If in their last moments, what they felt was finally free or guilty of many burdens. I believe it was an escape for them. Some will blame society, some will blame the person, some even blame neither. It depends though. I blame the voices in the persons head. They can get quite atrocious and loud sometimes. It's hard to hold on for far too long. I wonder if the voices fade at the end though, that is why a person can be finally free. Of their thoughts of everything.

Haunted House

I wrote this poem based on refugees who finally return to their countries after the dispute is cleared. It was sort of a perspective of how they feel. After doing quite a lot of research, I was confused as to why the patriotism was still there after all the terrible things that the country had done for them. After seeing the faces of the refugees and speaking of their country, it made me realize why it is called a home country itself. It is "home". It's your comfort place and where you can be your true self. It is where everyone is meant to allow you in and let you be yourself at the end of the day. What if the house you loved and cared about was shattered and broken to shreds though? The house that accepted you and comforted you. Let you grow, be raised, and gain fond memories suddenly mounds of junk. After returning from a temporary house to your so-called childhood, it was definitely not the house you once lived in. Yet, no matter who did this to your house or what happened to it. You can't hate this house. It is what once gave you joy so you still bleed for this house no matter what.

Endless Infinity

This poem was inspired based on the quote "nothing is impossible" which is very famous. People can laugh upon it, some can choose to live by it. Once more, I thought of it merely as a quote that was just motivation. Something to keep someone going, not a realistic quote but an inspiring one. Yet, one day when I sat down on my roof I looked at the sky above me. It wasn't filled with stars, it wasn't shiny or the moon didn't shine on me like I had expected it to. It was blank, empty and dull. The possibilities were endless though, even though the sky was lacking of the shining. It's a free world, a free universe, a free life. When you're trapped inside a box so small, living inside a bubble of only inside means, the vision outside gets so blurry and difficult to see that you find comfort in the bubble. There are far too many things to be discovered and to create. Infinite ends, infinite possibilities and I wondered why I was trapped in my box for so long. Stressing over the smallest things when there were millions of things reaching out to me. Allow it to be abstract, difficult to comprehend, confusing, mysterious. It's what makes life fascinating. I wrote this poem dedicating it to the curiosities and hidden depths of what's there to see, the endless infinity.

Lacuna

This poem was about what it was to felt "numb". Even after experiencing sadness, anger, joy, I felt like feeling numb was worse than all of the. You have no reason to feel numb, you don't know why you feel so. It's like feeling everything along with nothing at the same time. A mix of emotions rushing in all at once that makes you so overwhelmed that it makes you feel nothing, that is what I believe is being numb. Staying numb for too long is like feeling empty for ages. You cannot feel pain, you cannot feel happy. It's nothing. You question what to do in this numbness. Sing a song in joy? Sit in the emptiness of screech in pain? Anything to get rid of feeling nothing is better than being numb. That is why I believe being numb is worse than rest the feelings.

W Women, L 1964

I've been taught of discrimination against women at school, it's an issue. At first, it was silly fights such as "you can't do this because you're a girl". You think nothing of it because it's coming out of a child's mouth, I thought as I'd grow I'd see maturity. Now that I have grown, I still see it sometimes. I've been taught to dress neatly, but I always question why none of the boys have ever been taught to think neatly. Deep down inside, I know there's still something to be changed, to be fixed. Women possess great qualities and powers. The power of life, tolerance, and capability of going through pain. My mother goes through this everyday and I sincerely believe it should be valued and respected more.

Time Turns to Trees

This a poem based on a fear I have, one that gets me to shiver as I think of my place here in time, at this moment. I have written works for others, told stories to others, and given content to others. I wish to see them carry my writings alongside them, remember them and keep them protected as proof of my existence. Once I disperse, how long would it take for me to be forgotten? I wish that there may be someone who reads what I write, and understand the writings. It is what I believe is the greatest connection, a bond through words. No matter era, time, or place. I write words to feel connected, perhaps not understood, yet heard.

The tree; The Witness

I wrote this poem during the time I had witnessed a high and profound biases. I wouldn't prefer stating the name of the person. It's like being a painting displayed in the museum, one painted or sculpted by a different painter. Yet, everyone mostly goes to the most astounding painting. Why is it that painting was better, though? Sure, the artist was magnificent and the work was magnificent but so were all the other paintings as well. They had depth and meaning, yet why is it that there was only one painting getting more attention than the rest. I wanted to relate this to life in general, one gifted getting more attention and all the care taken. What about the rest? It was as though everyone forgot how to grow a plant. They watered the plant only after it bloomed, some though died without the watering. Others strived on rain, others had their leaves cut off, others plucked, and the most beautiful lot being admired. It was a saddened truth I found.

Obscure for sight

This was a poem based on depression. It's highly common these days, with the rates going up. I wanted to showcase it and display it through this poem. Feeling that everyone was shutting you out but at the same time, you're in desperate need to chat with someone. For me, having my room as an escape but also a cage was what I used to feel during those times. Sometimes, my thoughts became quite violent, scaring me too in fact. I started to fear what I was becoming, an ugly human being. Sometimes, crying too much leaves you numb so you get stinged and aches instead. There were ways to get rid of this pain. Yet the simplest one seemed the easiest yet it was the deadliest. Being held in those times, trying to escape it made me realise how obscure I was for the sight. Some sight given to me to awaken from that looping cycle.

The Solitary Man

There are times I've felt life to be endless yet dreadful. There is a particular cycle that I feel I follow every single day : To wake, To Work, To not question every choice, to see, and to sleep. Every single day this pattern followed me, making me find solace in my solitary. If I could do more than this, would I accept the challenge? Or had I already given up, accepting that this is all that will happen throughout the life that I lead. Just an average one, perhaps some exciting events, yet in the end I stay comforted in the fact that I am average. The solitary man is a sort of metaphor to show most of the working people in today's society, purely existing and promising to live later.

Pawn

In life, we're all labelled by status. In chess, it's the king, queen, rooks, bishops, knights, then the pawns. It's due to the value of the piece that makes us act upon the piece. For sure, the king has the highest value but isn't the king useless? To a more realistic view, is it the ones with most power who are more important or is it the ones with no power? I wanted to phrase the question differently by saying that the powerful ones depend on those who aren't powerful and vice versa. The pawns don't realise the strength and capability they have if they come together as a whole as it is them who ever placed the powerful there, isn't it?

Far-Fetched Forest

Guilt is a terrible thing to ever feel, it acknowledges your wrong. This poem is slightly based on any sort of guilty pleasure or doing something we know is wrong and can be adverse later on.

Mundane

In the end, even I myself question why I've written these poems. A reason, a thought, and a letter. Life doesn't always have to be sweet, I myself heard things that the poems were pessimistic, dull, dark and negative. I wanted to capture the bitter essence I found as I lived through my years, even if they may be pessimistic. I could never get myself to naturally do something so quickly like how I wrote these poems in a brisk way. They flowed to be like they were meant to be written, they came effortlessly. It's difficult for me to write about joyous things like spring, summer, flowers using poetry because I have too many thoughts held in my head still to be written. One day, I'd stop for a moment to breathe away this skill from me. Finally be at ease and content in life. Writing of the lush life and pristine nature, I don't think it'd ever make me resonate as much as I do with the mysteries of human nature.

Quest Of Time

The poem is of time. I've heard of the phrase "live in the present" quite often. I simply thought of it as something that is of the obvious but as time went by, soon I noticed it was never the case for me for far too long. Time has been taken advantage of multiple times. It has no value but at the same time has the most value. Sometimes, we recall only the past that shapes us. Our mistakes, regrets, faults, or the memories of glee, happiness, etc. We obsess about the past but we also obsess highly of the future. For me, every action I made questioned what would happen next. Afraid of letting loose and to in fact enjoy what I had. Instead, I chose to precisely live for the future while having moments I regretted in the past. Time must move, life must go on but yet, it's hard to catch up. You get left behind, run far too ahead. Rarely comes the time for me to walk along with the hands of the clock to enjoy the present. I hesitate for my future and remain guilty for my past, I never see the time lying right in front of me, soon walking away.

People Pleaser

When I was writing this poem, I wondered if I ever truly needed anyone. I believe it's a chapter in life where one can awaken and look at the people around them and question, are these really the right people? All the years I had lived, It was as though I wasn't indeed living for myself but for someone else to see. Like an item displayed in public for everyone to see, criticise, enjoy, or like. I tried and tried to make them all appreciate all of me. Though as much as I cared, comforted, and pushed myself all for their liking, in the end all the effort goes unbothered by a small incident. I for sure know many other people face this as well, it makes me wonder if I should have cared for it all in the first place, if in the end they'll all just turn their backs. Should I have remained? If given the chance, would I still be a people pleaser.

I Like Being Young

This poem doesn't have that much of a complex vocabulary or meaning as the other ones, it is also related to "burdened bagages". I didn't want to make this poem complex, how much I'd try to rephrase it, this was the most relatable way. I wanted to make this simple, comforting, and something young as it is about youth. In fact, we're all young souls so there's no need for me to break in the sweat for the old words and says. When you feel young, when you have youth, no one can take it away. I wanted to write about how it feels, to be young at such a time and place as someone young myself. I experienced joy and sadness throughout my years, including this year as well but for some reason, I liked it. I liked every inch and part of it.

MELIORISM

www.ingramcontent.com/pod-product-compliance
Lightning Source LLC
Chambersburg PA
CBHW022107040426
42451CB00007B/161